The
Art of
MAJORING
in Minor
Things

The
Art of
MAJORING
in Minor
Things

The Leadership
Challenge

Jules **Ciotta**

THE ART OF MAJORING IN MINOR THINGS
THE LEADERSHIP CHALLENGE

iUniverse books may be ordered through booksellers or by contacting:

iUniverse
1663 Liberty Drive
Bloomington, IN 47403
www.iuniverse.com
1-800-Authors (1-800-288-4677)

Because of the dynamic nature of the Internet, any web addresses or links contained in this book may have changed since publication and may no longer be valid. The views expressed in this work are solely those of the author and do not necessarily reflect the views of the publisher, and the publisher hereby disclaims any responsibility for them.

Any people depicted in stock imagery provided by Getty Images are models, and such images are being used for illustrative purposes only. Certain stock imagery © Getty Images.

ISBN: 978-1-5320-4369-7 (sc)
ISBN: 978-1-5320-4370-3 (e)

Print information available on the last page.

iUniverse rev. date: 03/12/2018

CONTENTS

To Trish, my wife. The best thing that ever happened to me. Thank you.

INTRODUCTION

Jules Ciotta is the son of immigrant parents, the oldest of three sons, growing up in a lower income family in an Italian and African American neighborhood.

Survival was the family's primary objective where doing good enough is good enough. One didn't have to be a high achiever. As long as one got by and didn't disgrace the family that was good enough.

Jules was the first person in the larger family that completed high school. Later, his two brothers and he would go on to complete advanced degrees.

What was highly important to the family and most families in the neighborhood was honesty, values, and integrity. Qualities that are missing in today's world. Doing something because it was the right thing to do.

Everyday media reports of cheating, lying, stealing, and taking advantage of those in lessor situations in life prevails. Even legal behavior can be wrong because it takes advantage of others in lesser positions.

The thought of writing a book on the inefficiency of management has been on the author's agenda for several years. Experience as an organizational psychologist working with many companies of all sizes, for over 30 years, gives him insight into the positioning of leaders in past and present work environments. The engagement in competitive sports and being an officer in the military helped the author realize that "being good enough was not good enough." Also, Napoleon Hill's book, "Think and Grow Rich" was life challenging for Jules. The position that "whatever the mind can conceive and believe becomes reality" is significant. Simply stated, "we're not what we think we are, but what we think, we are.

The increasing loss of values and character among today's management has made him recognize that he didn't have a choice. Managing by the art of majoring in minor things, saving the derriere, cover-ups, and putting out fires are the modes of getting things done today. These approaches are not limited to business leaders but are found among management in education, government, family, religion, and even the military.

Lack of accountability is the major problem in the world today. We've gotten away from "doing the right thing" because it's the right thing as in the past. One has to guard against letting the ego prevent him/her from being participatory when engaged with others.

This work provides skills that leaders can benefit from but more importantly, it highlights the need for each of us to be bolder in not tolerating mediocrity, holding others (even our management) accountable and not compromise our character and values. We need to do the right things regardless of the consequences, as reputation and integrity demands no less.

PREFACE

There are many books dealing with effective management, perhaps more appropriately referred to today as effective leadership. Sometimes differentiating between management and leadership in itself can be confusing. The manager is one who says, "There's what needs to be done, go do it." Whereas the leader takes the position, "There's what needs to be done, let's go do it." The difference of involvement is critical. There are many aspects to what management is and much written which gives rise to this confusion and it is confusing because it's difficult to effectively lead another. Oftentimes, it has been thought that because an individual has been effective in doing a job while on the line or as a member of the staff he/she will also be effective in a supervision or leadership role. The difference between effectively doing a job on the line and being effective in leading others is so diverse that there is no guarantee of success. There is an entirely different set of rules relative to one being effective in leading others. And this is the crisis that faces business.

The concern is how does one who is responsible for leading others involve him or herself in a way that will result in a positive environment that encourages others to commit to meeting organizational goals, the goals of the leader, and the goals that have been set forth for success to be achieved.

Why is it necessary, since there are so many books on the market dealing with management and leadership that another book be written and even though there's no way to stop chronicling additional thoughts and oftentimes duplicating them. So why is it necessary for this author to take time now to put those notes together? In a nutshell, this author believes there is a point missing that needs to be brought forth and that is, unequivocally stated, that the major difficulty or problem that exists today in American leadership in both public and private sectors, in both industrialized and non-industrialized environments, that prevents organizations from being even more effective than they are and to some extent they are effective, is that management itself is really weak. It is weak for several reasons, which we'll give thought to. Management accepts that once it gets into a position of authority in leading or managing others, it takes on an air of superiority which makes it difficult for the manager or leader to then be human enough to integrate with workers. He/she must be able to self-acknowledge the fact that they have limitations too and need to be involved on a horizontal rather than a vertical basis with those they're responsible for leading.

This is critical because it is not possible for a leader to know and understand his/her subordinates unless workers are provided the opportunity to utilize their creative and innovative abilities.

The manager or leader has to find a way of being able to recognize that the task is the boss, the boss is not the boss. The task is the boss and the person doing the job is the expert. The person doing the job has to be the one who does the job the best and the leader has a responsibility, in a form of orchestrating, to coach and counsel to ensure that the individual doing the job is on target. The leader needs enough insight and information about the responsibilities the individual has to perform to be able to hold this person accountable for doing his or her job without necessarily giving the impression that because I am the boss I know more than you do or you have to do it my way.

CHAPTER ONE

IT'S MINDSET THAT MATTERS

A leader's greatest struggle is within him or herself. Leaders need to realize that the organization's survival and success and their own depend upon effective leadership.

Talent, skill, experience, and even formal education, in themselves, do not guarantee success, positive mindset does. It's a positive mindset that matters most in today's high pressured and fast-paced business climate.

The role of the leader is changing and changing fast. The old "do it because I said so" model is crumbling and a more participatory approach is effectively taking its place.

We need to be more concerned about what our workers think, involve them more in the decision-making process, and let them know where what they do fits in. However, in doing so, leadership needs to be sure it doesn't lose control and sets up an environment of "no excuses-results" by being sure everyone knows they are in a work area where all are held accountable.

BUILDING A PLAYGROUND

Putting together an effectively running organization is like building a playground. Everyone on the playground needs to rally around ideas, be part of what's going on, and commit to working together to make it all happen.

Leaders need to step up with a positive mindset to ask, "What do we do now?" Meeting and thinking about what needs to be done next to lead to success. Experience has shown that when workers' minds and hearts are directed and involved in a project, participants will make the commitment to making it happen on the playground.

The process is most effective when all persons are involved. Those involved have ownership, are recognized for contributions made, leaders are in their proper place, and others outside the playground that have an interest or are affected are included.

Workers have fun on a playground. The work is challenging but provides a sense of importance and value on an environment of play. Expect a lot, get a lot … expect little and one won't be disappointed either.

POSITIVE DEMEANOR

The way we walk, talk, dress, drive a car, and just everything else we do expresses who we are and who we think we are. Oftentimes, this is referred to as "executive presence."

Understand that when what we say in words conflicts with what our body language is saying, our body language is more credible. Who we think we are manifests itself in the way we project ourselves and that is how others are judging us and thereby treating us.

Employees respond best to those they respect, and respect leaders who they perceive respect themselves and display respect to them. Each of us is the sum total of all our experiences and will not be the same person tomorrow that we are today.

Although it may not be noticeable from day-to-day, we will be a little more positive or negative tomorrow than we are today. That's why we need to continually work at maintaining control of who we are and what we do. Our executive demeanor is being affected by how we think of ourselves.

Successful people avoid saying and thinking "what they like to be" or "what their dreams are to be" but rather, say and think what they have decided "they're going to be."

There need not be any conceit to this, just a calm and assertive demeanor that comes from the heart. It is said with conviction and certainty that makes it believable.

There are those with extraordinary talent who do not achieve the level of success they desire and/or deserve. We manifest the things we desire in our lives with the power of our thoughts.

Our biggest obstacle to achieving success is ourselves by not creating positive thoughts and not focusing our attention on the things we desire.

ESTABLISH GOOD WORKPLACE

MBO, Managing by Objectives is an important part of holding workers accountable; however, MBWA is increasingly more important. Management by Wandering Around helps leaders to effectively engage with their workers more fully.

To make a commitment to their jobs, workers need to know that they belong, are valued, and making a contribution to the organization. They want to be part of a good workplace.

When employees of good workplaces are asked what makes their companies so good, they talk first about attractive benefits. But when you probe further, they all use terms like trust, pride, freedom, family, fairness, and fun. These almost universal descriptions of the atmosphere and the ways in which people work and relate to each other, indicate that good workplaces share certain qualities. They are:

- Friendly: Informal, pleasant, with a relative lack of social hierarchy.
- Not political: No constant jockeying for position or looking over your shoulder
- Fair: Employee complaints are heard impartially and fully
- More than a job: Employees have a role in defining their jobs, determining priorities, critiquing, and feeling that their company makes a valuable contribution to society that stands for something more than a business making a profit
- Like a family

Great workplaces implicitly say people tend to work more cooperatively when they are treated with respect, given a say in what they do, and given what they consider a fair share of the rewards for their efforts. That may require disturbing managers' traditional role, but it is a non-manipulative answer to the mystery of motivation.

Without profits, a private enterprise will die. But what is important about a great workplace is that profits are not something to be achieved at the expense of the people responsible for creating them. A great workplace suggests that it's possible to achieve that success while enriching the lives of the people who work there.

EXPLAIN THE RULES

Although all workplaces have rules, leaders need to be sure employees have the mindset to learn and know them.

There are particularly good times to be sure rules are clearly understood. Orientation is a particularly good time to let new employees know what behavior is expected with supporting written documentation of the rules.

When changes in rules are made, they need to be communicated. It is best for them to be communicated both verbally and in writing. Workers should at this time be encouraged to ask questions. Leaders need to demonstrate their openness to comments and suggestions so they will feel free to share them.

When a rule is broken, immediate action is needed to let the worker know that such behavior is prohibited and why. This action must be done verbally and followed up in writing.

When a violation of a rule takes place in a public setting, reserve reprimand and discussion until you can get the individual to a private location.

A rule which is not immediately corrected will not only continue but will get worse. Some broken rules that are not acted upon and witnessed by other workers will encourage them to break the same rules.

MAKING WORKERS FEEL NEEDED

While conducting a leadership workshop at a contact lens company, the author spoke with a cleaning woman while she was preparing to provide coffee for a meeting in an adjoining room.

The woman was approximately 35 years of age, attractive, Hispanic, and very shy. Jules gave her his name and asked her for hers. After saying, Marilyn, she was asked what she would do if she were a boss. She responded by saying she would genuinely ask workers what they think would make things even better because workers want to feel a part of what is going on. Marilyn was thanked for her comment and Jules told the 14 leaders in the workshop that started 10 minutes later about this encounter and Marilyn's answer. They were surprised because of their perception that lower level workers are not that aware of what is going on, but they are.

Jules followed the conversation by asking if anyone knew what her name was and not one of them did. She was not important enough to find out her name although she is commonly seen working in the building.

Interestingly, two months later, while walking from the parking lot to the manufacturing building, Jules heard his name called out from a higher area, 40 yards away. He returned the greeting and walking toward the building he realized that the call was Marilyn's way of saying thank you for making me feel important. Workers will oftentimes forget what leaders say but they never forget how they make them feel.

IMPROVING MINDSET

Mindset can be improved by having an influence on how others perceive the quality of who we are as an organization. Workers need to understand the importance of a positive mindset and as leaders; we see them as our customers.

As our customers, we are exceeding their expectations that we are continuously improving by pursuing total quality, increasing speed and agility, and embracing change. We need and expect them as our staff to join us in doing the same. We are in this work environment together, let's make it happen now.

A positive mindset on behalf of the leader, releases the creativity and power of workers by empowering employees, training and re-training them, and rewarding good performance.

GETTING THROUGH TO THE WORKFORCE

To communicate effectively with your workforce, leaders need to understand their preconceptions and expectations.

Here are some of the viewpoints that leaders would benefit from understanding:

- **Treat us like we're stupid.** Workers know what is going on and want to be brought in on what is going on from their leaders.
- **Leaders have all the answers.** Be honest with workers rather than acting like we are without error. Be honest and human in communications.
- **Too busy to listen.** Leaders need to avoid getting so busy in their jobs that they do not have time to mix with their workers. Workers need involvement from their leaders and to be actively listened to.
- **We are smarter than you think.** Their perception is that workers know a lot less than they do and are not as smart as they are. Leaders need to challenge and more effectively utilize their creativity.
- **We want to believe.** Workers want to believe the best about the organization they work for. They want to be given the reasons to believe things are improving in the organization. With this, their attitudes will improve accordingly.

DO FOR YOURSELF

As narcissistic as it seems, we cannot do for another what we cannot first do for ourselves. One has to love him or herself before being able to love another because the love we can give ourselves determines our capacity to love another.

The challenge that most people face is that they know what they want, but oftentimes have a hard time focusing on the action steps to get there. It's difficult to have a long term focus when our lives are filled with diversions and distractions.

Key to overcoming this challenge is to make the commitment that everything in your life you're responsible for.

Now we know that others and circumstances can cause our problem; however, when we can say and feel that "I'm responsible," we're in control.

It's not what happens to us in life that's important, what's important is how we perceive it. When I take responsibility I can take the necessary steps to change and/or correct the situation. Otherwise, I have to wait for who is responsible to take the action I want.

MISSING INGREDIENT IN MINDSET

Most people live in their past and the anticipation of their future. They would be happier and have more meaning in their lives if they lived in the moment.

"Happiness doesn't come from the celebration of victory but rather from the enjoyment of the game." It is not possible for us to achieve all our goals in life yet if we did, we could still miss out on life itself. We need to have a worthwhile purpose in life and live in the present.

As Voltaire put it, "Do not anxiously expect what has not yet come. Do not vainly regret what has already past." As Eckhart Tolle states in his book *The Power of Now*, "Live in the moment. We can learn from yesterday, plan some for tomorrow, but be ever conscious of living in the moment, the now."

In his book, *The Master Game*, Robert de Ropp states, "Seek, above all, for the game worth playing. Having found the game, play it with intensity. Play as if your life and sanity depended on it, because they do." It's mindset that matters!

CHAPTER TWO

Communications – Getting the Message Across

Communications is the flow or interchange of information, thoughts, and opinions between a transmitter and a receiver.

It has been said that "it's not what you say but what you mean to say that's important." That is true but it is not enough because feedback is needed to be sure the receiver understands what you said. To be most effective, leaders need to communicate horizontally, not vertically. Asking for suggestions from staff will make workers feel involved in the decision which results in commitment from workers. The leader does not have to accept all suggestions for commitment to occur.

SHARING THE POWER HELPS TO DEVELOP THE STAFF

We are, each of us, the sum total of all our experiences. One problem and/or situation affects us in others. When employees feel strong, involved and needed, they get extraordinary things done while those who feel weak and insignificant consistently underperform and want to flee.

People who feel powerless tend to hoard the power they have. For example, powerless leaders usually adapt petty and dictatorial styles where political skills are utilized. "Covering your rear" and "passing the buck" are modes used to handle difficulties. Powerless employees tend to follow orders and avoid taking any initiative.

Sharing power is the answer. It lets workers know they are responsible for doing their own jobs – doing what they are paid to do – to help the organization succeed. It helps management and non-management realize the need not "to major in minor things" and continue to ensure that accountability is part of the day-to-day operation.

Methods that should be incorporated to ensure this approach is being effectively applied include the following modes:

- **Develop competence**. The growth of all workers is the leader's second mission.
- **Provide choice**. Allow workers the opportunity to make suggestions knowing that they will be listened to and taken seriously.
- **Ensure self-leadership**. Let workers know they are the experts in doing their own jobs and are accountable to themselves, you, and the organization.
- **Offer visible support**. Workers generally want more room; let them know they have it…additional rope is also capable of hanging them.

This approach is most effective in moving an organization forward. It lets people know they are held in dignity, are provided with specific and challenging shared responsibilities and will be held accountable for meeting them.

LEADERS NEED TO GET OUT OF THEIR IVORY TOWERS

I remember when working with a major newspaper organization and suggesting that top management needed to change two things they were doing. They regularly ate in the executive dining room rather than the company lunch room. I suggested that they mix with workers in the lunch room and utilize the dining room for entertaining visitors and special occasions. In addition, they were asked to remove reserved executive parking and make it available on a job need basis. Make it available to those who come and go like advertising and circulation department staffs.

When revisiting this organization a month later, the leaders were mixing with the staff in the lunch area more often. The parking situation remained the same with the excuse that some concession was made.

START COACHING AND NOT MANAGING

As a whole, American management is so wrapped up in its own agenda that it doesn't have time for, or doesn't care about the development of people. Companies are filled with managers who are totally indifferent to their employees. The corporations are loaded with managers with superior attitudes, poor interpersonal skills, and poor listening/feedback skills. Add the fact that managers also have trouble delegating, developing employees, or conducting performance evaluations, and the problem comes into focus.

The manager's ego can also often cause him/her to have a short fuse, being impatient and critical of the employee, not the work. This all adds up to low morale and productivity, which leads to poor quality products and/or services and higher costs.

Successful organizations have leaders who coach, not manage... leaders to integrate the company's effort in a shared leadership style that gives everyone ownership. Workers are generally, waiting to be challenged and would respond in kind. As a rule, the manager's ego prevents the ability to "let go" thereby creating a micromanaged and bureaucratic organization. The dictatorial work environment, which doesn't provide for shared leadership and individual growth, is limiting the company's success for the sake of top management.

Downsizing and other methods to take away from the dignity of the worker will reap, and will continue to reap, low morale and company failures.

Business cannot be done as it was in the past, and those who make the decisions have to insure that all the energy and creative spirit of all workers is utilized. If workers are not encouraged to participate without concern for consequences of failure, management will be left to "play God" and fail to get the best from the employees. Although there are times when dictatorial management has short-term success, it usually fails in the long term.

When workers are made to feel important and valued, they work harder and do a better job. They wake up in the morning and say: I'm happy to go to work today because I'm needed and appreciated.

When they are managed with trust, they turn their work into fun. Workers who are effectively motivated:

- Are glad to see their leaders
- Smile more
- See themselves as the company
- Are eager to make eye contact
- Enjoy talking with their bosses

THE LEADERSHIP VOID

In the complex work environment we are in today, managers are forgetting about the most important aspect of their jobs, leading their teams. The jobs of managers are getting so crunched that they are too often neglecting their direct reports.

Employees become frustrated with their work environment when they feel like they have no direct leadership, so leaders need to find ways to refocus their efforts on setting a good example for their teams.

Get into the trenches:

Whatever it is that your team does on a daily basis, do it with them as much as you can. Whether it's cold-calling prospects or writing promotional copy, if you want to become an effective leader, then team members have to feel like they can identify with what you do. Employees too often complain that their managers don't understand how hard their jobs are. Take that complaint away by joining them.

Have one-on-one meetings:

These can't be checkup, Big Brother-type meetings, but rather should be as open as possible. Let your employees vent about things that are bothering them or simply talk about the latest deals they're trying to close. Everyone wants a team leader who is eager to listen to them. Find time to do it.

CULTURE OF COLLABORATION

Effective organizations rely on employees working together, making a commitment, and taking responsibility. A culture of openness, cooperation, collaboration, and continuous improvement is thus vital to long-term success.

Employees need to be encouraged to acquire new attitudes and work habits that will allow them to fully contribute to the process to which they belong.

Workers must be empowered for the new design to work. The new organization depends on progress groups to work together and make decisions without resorting to approval from a hierarchy or managers. However, employees must have the necessary tools, the important and timely information, as well as the authority to make these decisions. Training is also key to the success of empowering people

The horizontal organization rejects the placement of people and work into functional departments. Instead, it groups people and work around a few organization-wide, cross-functional core processes. All processes lead to one end objective: Creating and delivering something of value to the customer.

CREATE A SUGGESTION ENVIRONMENT

There are ways we can get results from an employee suggestion program. A work environment that makes employees feel willing to volunteer suggestions needs to be established.

Letting employees know what will happen to their ideas with a flowchart, which shows the process would help them make suggestions.

Providing a general idea of how long a typical response takes and giving employees easy to understand categories they could give suggestions in. Morale, cost cutting, and interdepartmental communications are examples.

LISTENING IS VITAL

Do you listen to your employees? Really listen? Letting employees talk is not the same as listening. You have to work at it, the same way you work at anything else you want to succeed at.

1. **Put your work away.** As soon as an employee comes to you and wants to talk, put away whatever you're working on. Remove all temptations to do anything.
2. **Bite your tongue.** One of the first signs that someone isn't listening is when he or she cuts off the talker in midsentence or mid-thought. Make sure your employee is finished before you begin speaking.
3. **Smile and lean forward.** You'll be amazed at the effect a simple smile can have. By smiling and leaning forward, you send the message that you're fully engaged in what the person is saying.
4. **Always ask questions, even if you don't have any.** Questions tell the employee that you've been listening, and are truly committed to resolving whatever issue is being discussed.
5. **Start your own comments by paraphrasing the employee.** Again, this tells the employee that you've been listening; it also helps you get the issues clear in your own head before you speak your thoughts.

GOOD COMMUNICATIONS BUILDS GREATNESS

The organization that gives importance to creating an open, communicating climate throughout the environment helps it build and maintain systems and procedures which lead to sound decisions. It builds trust among individuals and grows and brings problem-solving responsibilities as close to the information source as possible.

GREATNESS IS WITHIN

Greatness lies within every organization. Effective communications, making workers feel that they are needed, belong, and are valued is the vital difference; it nurtures this greatness into reality. The spirit of workers, leaders, and the organization, as a whole, moves toward productivity results that are consistent with goals and mission. Through this kind of communication, all benefit.

Experience indicates that building trust in individuals is vital to effective leadership. As love in a marriage, trust in the workplace holds people together to get good results. To build trust, we need to make ourselves vulnerable by setting aside the masks we oftentimes wear and let our real selves be known. Other workers know we're human and would appreciate our being more comfortable about this fact.

We can also build trust by taking risks on behalf of our co-workers.

CHAPTER THREE

MANAGING BY WANDERING AROUND

Management consultant, Tom Peters wrote that as important as MBO (Managing by Objectives) is to leaders, MBWA (Managing by Walking Around) is more important."

It is clear that workers want to be involved, be part of the process, and make a difference. To the degree that leaders can make the worker feel that he/she plays an important role, he/she will respond.

WORKERS ARE OFTENTIMES UNDERVALUED

Working with a New Jersey printing plant, the Board of Trustees hired me to assess and improve the relationship between the president and vice president and the morale in the plant.

To kick off the program, I held a meeting with the workers in the plant. The only place we could get everyone together. The two executives were on each side of me as I addressed the group letting them know that something was going to be done to improve the work environment.

After my comments and a few words from both the president and vice president, I asked for questions and comments from the group. All but one person were too intimidated to comment. The one person who did, made significant and useful suggestions which I recorded and thanked him for.

While returning to the administrative offices with the president, I learned that the person who shared his thoughts was one of the janitors.

There is a tendency for leaders to believe that workers, particularly in lower positions, don't know what is going on, but they do. They also want to do something to make the work environment better but often do not have the opportunity.

Many times when workers get involved in community activities like Little League, Girl Scouts, and the PTA, it is because they have an energy that is not being effectively utilized in their jobs.

MAKE RECOGNIZING EMPLOYEES A DAILY ROUTINE

Good managers remember to recognize and motivate employees. Great leaders do it every day. Here are some proven methods for making sure that praising employees becomes part of your daily routine:

- **Make employees a part of your weekly "to do" list.** Add the names of the people who report to you to your list of goals to accomplish. Then cross off names as you praise them.
- **Use voice mail.** Rather than using it only to assign tasks, leave employees voice mail messages praising them for a job well done. Do it from your cellular phone on the way home.

- **Write notes at the end of the day**. Keep a stack of note cards on your desk, where you can't ignore them. At the end of the day, take a minute to write a thank you note to any employee who made a difference that day.
- **At the beginning of the day, put five coins in your pocket**. Then, during the day, each time you praise an employee, transfer a coin to your other pocket. It may sound corny, but once you get in the habit, you'll start relying on tricks like this one.

LEADERS VERSUS MANAGERS

Good leaders lead by example. They are role models. They convey a vision and a mission. They encourage, teach, coach, and inspire others to great achievement. They deal with crises. They seem instinctively to know what to do when the stuff hits the fan. They lead people.

Managers work on the specifics of the job. They pay attention to the numbers. Managers plan and direct. They make sure everything goes smoothly and as projected. Leaders spell out what to do while a manager makes sure it gets done.

Leaders recruit the right players and help everyone determine where they need to go., slide into the driver's seat, and head the bus, to use Jim Collins' analogy in "*Good to Great*," toward everyone's goal. Managers slip into the back of the bus, count heads, and watch the road for bumps and other hazards.

PRINCIPLES BEHIND SUCCESSFUL COACHING

Coaching is not the same as managing. There are specific principles that make it different from traditional managing.

To be an effective coach, let employees know that they have the ability to do better. They may need encouragement or training but you have the confidence in their ability. Also, let them know that they know more than they think they know and you'll probe them until they prove it to themselves.

As a coach, give your people open-ended questions to get them included. This is better than giving commands and finding fault. Remember that even setbacks are learning opportunities. Rather than punishment, as a coach, identify the causes and consequences of setbacks.

Challenges bring out the best in workers so find and provide exciting and attainable challenges that stretch workers skills to help them be the best they can be.

Employees who can feel comfortable doing things, even when experiencing failure, are going to learn and grow.

SET A GOOD EXAMPLE

Like it or not, people tend to look to their leadership to determine their behavior. To inspire employees and command respect, always speak and act in the organizations best interest. A few tips to help us lead by example follow:

- **Treat everyone with respect and graciousness.** Everyone you work with – from your biggest customer to the maintenance crew – contributes to your organization's success. Keep that in mind when greeting them in the hall, answering a question, or talking with them at organization functions.

- **Put your clients on a pedestal.** Begin staff meetings by talking about how the organization solved a problem for a client or customer. Constantly remind staffers that their job is to serve customers, no matter what their job titles are.
- **Refer to the mission statement frequently.** Employees look to managers to give their day-to-day work purpose and meaning. One of the best ways to do that is to take every opportunity to remind people of the organization's mission. When announcing a business decision, for example, use the mission to explain your decision.
- **Tie everything to goals.** Even when delivering criticism, tie your comments back to the organization's goals. Saying "you need to redo the illustrations on the brochure to reflect our commitment to diversity" improves employees' understanding of your organization's priorities.
- **Don't complain about the organization** to employees or clients. It sets a bad example, and destroys your credibility.

LEADERSHIP TAKES WORK AND THE RESULTS ARE WORTH IT

Leadership incubates over time through training, observing, mentoring and, yes, having some innate abilities. The time was when people believed that leadership was the product of nature – leaders were born, not made. Today, management specialists agree that nurture and environment both combine to produce effective leaders. With wise selection and effective training, organizations can groom promising leaders, even those who may not demonstrate natural leader talents.

Many aspiring leaders adopt behaviors they observe other leaders using, whether or not the behaviors are right for the situation. No matter how you rate your leadership qualities, you should continuously renew and improve your skills. Without renewal, you tend to get stale, practicing a leadership style more habitual than situational. Renewal suggests examining your actions in light of your work climate and choosing the best leadership behavior for the situation.

Most of us know that effective leadership underlies business success, along with a clear vision, a good business plan, and the gut to push through adversity without letting the competition see you sweat. When you strive to accomplish your business goals, it is leadership that provides clarity and direction – or not.

In today's business environment, intense and constantly shifting changes confront organizations. Unrelenting change has become the norm, pressuring and complicating most aspects of business, and creating challenges bigger than before. As a result, organizations must develop exceptional leaders who can skillfully navigate the complex, ever changing business environment.

Organizations are people using tools, processes and knowledge to produce the goods and services valued by customers. How well these social and technical systems mesh determine the effectiveness of any organization.

Many organizations are out of balance because they emphasize the technical over the social system, particularly organizations that produce products. The truth is you can trace many business failures to a breakdown in social skills – skills that include, managing change, coaching employees, resolving conflicts, and communicating goals and strategy, to name a few.

LET GO OF YOUR NEED TO CONTROL

Letting go and letting our people decide is most difficult for managers. The perception is to tell workers what to do and then be sure they do it.

A coach can learn to effectively guide their workers through what needs doing by asking open-ended questions, actively. Listening, and sharing his/her own experiences.

Probing with open-ended questions, even when the feedback is disagreed with, encourages the worker to feel a part of the involvement. It also gives evidence that you can listen actively while asking questions to help clarify the employee's position on the matter helps.

This scenario can be enhanced by the coach sharing similar tasks in the past, even those where there was discomfort and where mistakes were made.

Leaders need to let go to grow. Not being able to let go limits growth on both the part of the worker and the coach.

BE CAREFUL

According to a Chinese proverb… Be careful with your thoughts for they become your words. Be careful with your words for they become your actions. Be careful with your actions for they become your character. Be careful with your character for it becomes your destiny.

YANKEE INGENUITY

There is a story of a toothpaste company that had an unusual problem. Consumers would find one or two tubes of toothpaste boxes empty in each large box of 24. To correct the problem, a consulting company, at considerable cost, installed a scale on the conveyor belt at the location prior to boxing the product. When an empty box passed over the scale, a bell would go off and one of two workers working nearby would remove the box from the conveyor belt.

Workers would laugh every time the bell would sound, saying "We got another one." After a few weeks the problem did not recur and the bell no longer sounded.

When the general manager investigated, he found that the workers who were responsible for removing the empty boxes got tired of doing so and secured the funds to purchase a $59.95 fan to take care of the problem.

The fan was placed prior to the scale and blew on the boxes as they passed along the line. Without enough weight, the empty boxes were blown off the conveyor belt which solved the problem at a price less than the thousands of dollars initially spent. Let's call this "Yankee Ingenuity."

STEPS TO MANAGING BY WANDERING AROUND

A leader who makes regular visits to his work environment can stay on top of what's going on and find ways to correct things.

Here are steps to how to make this work:

1. Give your employees notice that you will be doing this
2. Obtain basic knowledge on current problems and write it down
3. Make personal connections to build relationships during the rounds

4. Mention issues noted during previous visits and what's been or being done about it
5. Keep tone and words positive
6. Assure those presenting problems that they will be given your attention
7. Record issues that arise
8. Recognize/reward those providing useful information
9. Manage by Wander Around regularly so momentum isn't lost

FOCUS ON RESULTS

Organizations have tried hard to find ways of being more productive. Despite corporate coaching, Total Quality Management (TQM) and all forms of reengineering, most companies are still getting bogged down in bureaucracy, preventing focusing and results.

Successful companies should need only a few managers to take highly skilled people, focus their efforts, and give them responsibility for results.

Here are some steps for the organization committed to successfully moving forward:

1. Expedite. Mission Statements and even Vision Statements in themselves do little to get results. The key to getting the job done is to ensure that workers have the knowledge and skills to do the job right and the mindset to need to get it done well and on time. The ability to expedite is rare in today's workplace where people take little responsibility for their behavior and "major in minor things."
2. Results Oriented. Organizations need to be clearer about what they want and where they're going. Truly effective

companies are involving employees in determining goals and directions. Since communication is difficult to consistently maintain at an effective level, it is vital that decisions be communicated to employees to avoid multiple agendas, resulting in lack of focus.

3. Decision Making. Today's quick pace requires that decisions, too, be made quicker. To do this, organizations need to reduce layers and sign-offs. Reduce the time it takes normally to make decisions in an organization by reducing the amount of time taken in redundant meetings, memo passing, and procrastination.

Although these steps are not utopian, they can make a difference in cutting down on the morass that generally prevents real progress from taking place.

CHAPTER FOUR

CONFLICT IS INEVITABLE

Conflict is an everyday occurrence. Conflict will occur. The question is how effectively will we deal with it.

Our level of security determines how we will deal with conflict. It is not what happens to us in life that is important. How we deal with it is.

Amazingly our personalities are formed from our early years. Those people, parents, grandparents, siblings, and others determined what our personality is today. To effectively deal with conflict is to realize that when one gets upset about what someone said or did, there is need to recognize that I'm not really angry at what was said and happened. I'm angry at myself for not being able to effectively deal with it.

WHAT SETS WINNERS APART?

Oftentimes we think winners are just lucky. They were at the right place at the right time or born in the right family. However, experience tells us that there are things winners do that have made them successful.

Winners have a single purpose that is integrated into who they are and all that they do. This mindset helps them avoid wasting their time and lives majoring in minor things. This makes it possible for them to clearly understand who we are and where we're going.

Decision making is easier for one with a single purpose. Winners develop habits that give importance to integrity, values, commitment, accountability, and creativity. These habits create a character that puts emphasis on "the time is now." The winner clearly defines what is wanted and makes a full commitment to develop what it will take to obtain it. Winners make it happen while others spend their time and effort on waiting for it to happen.

Several years ago, I recall having dinner with the president of a printing company and his family. The president was upset and embarrassed by something his seven and one half year old son was doing. He was an energetic young man who was having trouble sitting. He scolded him telling him to sit down and not get up again. The unhappy boy responded by saying, "maybe you're going to get me to sit down on the outside, but on the inside, I'm still standing up."

When leaders force their will on workers without providing understanding and reason, the workers may have no choice but to do it on the outside without making the commitment from the inside.

A POSITIVE SPIRIT KEEPS COMMITMENT AND MORALE UP

Accountability, values, commitment, and integrity have something in common. They each contribute to an organization being more successful in a work environment where others find it easy to pull back and play it safe at a time when "taking intelligent risks is the answer to succeeding."

Leaders need to be trained to create positive work teams that take on a "we can do it" mindset to more effectively take on today's challenges while preparing to be positioned to take on the future's upturn.

CREATING A LEARNING ENVIRONMENT

To remain competitive, we need to learn faster to keep pace with the sizzling pace of change.

As we have learned to upgrade our computers, we must also learn the importance of increasing the knowledge of our workforce. A generous training budget should be accepted as a basic cost of doing business.

There is need for a change in environmental mindset between the leaders and workers. The new approach needs to be "We'll help you grow in job enrichment and enlargement and in return you'll need to help the organization grow."

A big aspect of success is the ability to "keep going." This sounds simple but it's not because most people find excuses to stop their forward motion; sometimes before they even get started.

When one gets excited about what one is doing and begins enjoying it, the thought of stopping never occurs to him/her.

Things will not always go right, we will do dumb things, but one needs to just keep going. These circumstances will eventually make us wise. Apply this mindset and you will see yourself through situations, while growing, to the successful completion of the effort.

The 80-20 rule makes an important point, even though its accuracy is questionable. It states that 80% of people are going through life waiting for it to happen and 20% are making it happen. Experience states people are generally not bold enough to set forth and make it happen.

When leaders tell me he/she can't do it, I tell them they're right. If I'm told they can do it, my answer is the same. The law of expectations applies. We get from life, certainly from our work, pretty much what we expect.

DON'T BE AFRAID OF FEAR

What one needs to fear is not doing something well. If we try and fail and keep doing the same thing over and over again, "you can't solve a problem with the same mindset that created it."

There's no neutral, no coasting, and no sideways in life. In life, relationships, business, and spiritual growth, there's only up and down.

It's not unusual to "just want to get by." It's not such a big deal. Since there's only up and down, this mindset is a myth, an illusion. It means one is teetering on the edge of happiness, health, and contentment. This really means that the "do nothing to change" scenario life will likely be somewhere between unpleasant and dead.

So how should we deal with fear and not fear it? By realizing that failing produces the opportunity to succeed by getting up when falling down and moving forward knowing what didn't work.

The next time you feel that sideways, coasting, and/or neutral is enough, say "no it's not" and move positively forward.

ENERGIZE THE WORK ENVIRONMENT

Leaders need to make a conscious effort to create a work environment that is both productive and enjoyable for workers to come to. Providing techniques that more effectively utilizes employee energy is rewarded with committed, motivated, and productive workers who infect co-workers and customers in positive ways.

To have an energized work environment, leaders need to give attention to building morale, empowering their people, communicate horizontally, solicit suggestions from them, endorse creativity, and train while challenging workers.

Leaders who are secure and confident enough to establish a shared leadership work environment will find that their workers will not only make decisions about already set plans, but will set the plans themselves. This frees leadership to focus on other areas of growth for the organization.

Here are some things leaders can do to help process a mindset change:

1. Acknowledge the employee as an individual
2. Share information with employees
3. Help employees set career goals and action plans for achieving growth
4. Promote from within
5. Keep management doors open
6. Find assignments that help employees grow
7. Give employees greater responsibilities as their skills grow

8. Be honest
9. Help employees navigate the political by-ways
10. Recognize outstanding achievement
11. In team-based organizations, recognize and reward individual accomplishments with teams
12. Become more aware of the personal needs of your employees

Expect a lot from your people and get a lot; expect little and you won't be disappointed either.

HANDLING CHANGE EFFECTIVELY

People don't like change. We tend to get comfortable with what we're doing and want to leave it that way. Yet, growing requires change. In fact, we need to "Let go to grow."

When we become comfortable, we stop challenging ourselves to do and make it better. We need to continually work at making it better since we cannot stand still. If we're not moving forward, we're moving backward.

GUIDELINES TO EFFECTIVELY COACHING

There are guidelines that can help the leader reduce conflicts and coach workers to master complicated techniques and memorizing rules. There are basic guidelines that help leaders develop the habits and mindset that bring out the best from their staff.

First, the leader must show confidence in his/her staff to inspire them to make a concentrated effort to learn. The instruction also needs to be flexible because everyone will not be turned on to the same learning approach. The content needs to be the same; the process needs to be varied to meet individual personalities.

The leader needs to be a model of responsible behavior. The coach needs to do what he/she is teaching and promoting what is expected from others.

It is also beneficial, where possible, to give employees options. This avoids giving hard and fast orders, which tend to be resisted. When a mistake is made, don't respond with criticism until you know why the mistake was made and then coach the individual in how to avoid this kind of mistake in the future.

EFFECTIVELY DEALING WITH CONFLICT

We become more efficient leaders and coaches when we learn to welcome change, even welcome conflict. Accepting that change is inevitable and can, with the proper mindset, be to the advantage of not only oneself but the organization. Change can be used to charge up the organization. That's because change opens up doors to people's hearts and minds that otherwise might stay forever locked. The secret is to meet people at their point of need.

You must manage to the moment ... bring what's missing ... repair what change has damaged or destroyed. And you need to move quickly because high-velocity change puts heavy demands on the organization. You need people who invest themselves fully in their work, people who deliver dramatic results.

Basically, it comes down to this—you need to build a burning level of job commitment, and you need to do it by yesterday. In today's world of work, you can't afford to tolerate a commitment level that remains at room temperature.

CHAPTER FIVE

THE ORGANIZATION'S PERSONALITY AND DIRECTION

An organization is not brick and mortar, but the sum total of the personality of its people. An organization's success, in good part, results more from the mix of the work environment and the utilization of human and other resources than the value of the product and /or service itself.

ENERGIZING THE WORK ENVIRONMENT

With a winning attitude, leaders can create a work environment that is productive and also enjoyable to work in. By employee techniques that both grow and maintain workers energy, leadership is rewarded with committed employees who are motivated to get the job done and done well.

There are things that can be done to ensure that an energized work environment is established and maintained:

- Communicate – keep workers informed on what's going on and what they say is taken seriously
- Ask for suggestions - let workers know that what they say is important
- Empower people – let workers have more input in the decision making process
- Encourage creativity - invite workers to think outside the box
- Train workers - keep up ongoing training programs to develop workers
- Build morale - let workers know when they're doing a good job
- Challenge workers – stretch workers to more fully use their talents, they'll love it

Sharing leadership is not only a step toward empowerment but can give workers more control over their work. This also frees leaders to give attention to new areas of growth.

The well-known mystic, Eckhart Tolle writes of the importance of living in the now when he states:

"The division of life into past, present, and future is mind-made and ultimately illusory. Past and future are thought forms, mental abstractions. The past can only be remembered now. What you remember is an event that took place in the now, and you remember it now. The future, when it comes, is the now. So the only thing that is real, the only thing that ever is, is the now."

While consulting a major software company, I recall suggesting the company slow down selling their products. Although that's contrary to good business, there was a good reason for the suggestion.

The company's trainers, who provided how to utilize purchased products could not keep up with sales which was causing a major customer service problem. There is an Asian proverb which says "Don't let the head get so far ahead of the tail that it breaks in the middle."

The top executives did not pay attention to this advice and the company had serious financial problems which it overcame but the disappointment resulted in the company being sold.

SLOW DOWN WHEN YOU GET BUSIER

Slowing down when you get busier doesn't make any sense and yet it does. If you don't evaluate why you're so busy, the day could slip away without any meaningful accomplishment.

We can believe that the busier we are and the more complex things are, the more importance we have. Yet, something has its most complete state when it's in its simplest form.

So, concentrate on what really matters and give priority to that to do your best. Stop moving the small stuff from your list and get to what really matters.

By doing this, you will get away from doing as much busywork in favor of doing what's more important.

COMMON MISTAKES LEADERS MAKE

The most common complaints that employees express about their management need attention. Leaders have to give attention to things they can do to form a better working relationship, which leads to more effective work performance.

Complaint #1: Micromanaging. Good workers want the freedom to do their best work, not having the boss looking over their shoulder.

Solution: Provide defined avenues in a clear and specific way up front; giving room, monitoring progress, while the task is being completed.

Complaint #2: Doesn't understand what I do. The opposite of micromanaging. When employees believe the leader doesn't understand their roles, they can get cynical or defensive.

Solution: Take time to talk with employees about their activities. Stay close to show support and hold them accountable.

Complaint #3: Always flip flopping on decisions. Indecision and inconsistent leaders are hard to work for.

Solution: Develop core strategies and fixed objectives with the staff. Decide which objectives are more fixed and which are flexible. The leaders and staff can then work together to get them done.

Complaint #4: Talking about one employee to another. This is destructive behavior which any good leader knows needs to be stopped to be effective.

Solution: Bring the issue to the attention of the worker him/herself, without involving others in peer issues.

THE ORGANIZATION'S PERSONALITY

The organization's personality is the sum total of its mission, goals, objectives, beliefs, values, and attitudes. They determine our decisions, policies, and the course of our actions. Good organizations find ways to not let the personality be determined solely by the CEO, but provide as many opportunities for employee input.

Experience shows that leaders not only need to keep a balance between their jobs and their personal lives, but also to be balanced in their leadership posture.

By mindset, personality, and other factors resulting from the fact that we are the sum total of all our experiences, leaders will lean more toward being autocratic or passive. The more aggressive leader puts emphasis on being direct and uncompromising. This could and oftentimes does result in those working for him/her to behave passively aggressive, limiting their creativity, and waiting for it to happen rather than making it happen.

In contrast, the leader who is compassionate due to the need to be liked can lose sight of the goal and this oftentimes results in lack of accountability, focus, and an excuse filled work environment.

The truly successful leader has the skills and self-confidence to provide a balanced approach by being sure that everyone, including self, is specifically accountable while letting employees know they are valued and important to the organization's success. Workers are held with dignity in a clearly defined line of expectations that will be maintained.

Effective leaders continually make the effort to keep this balance because it's for the betterment of the organization, leader, and employee. It's a win/win situation.

Today, it is necessary to throw old rules for doing business out the window and develop new leadership ideas and techniques to move your organization forward.

In fact, the key to the success of any organization depends on leadership. Leadership matters most in today's fast moving, high pressure business climate. The executives and organizations that do things right will prosper, others are likely to fail. Since the role of the leader is changing, the dictatorial style of the past is crumbling and the style of strategist, coach, facilitator, cheerleader, and team builder is taking its place.

CHAPTER SIX

ACCOUNTABILITY IS VITAL TO SUCCESS

Every business and personal environment needs to give importance to accountability. A person needs to be accountable to self and a leader needs to be sure that he/she as well as workers are accountable. Without it, chaos will reign.

HOLDING STAFFERS ACCOUNTABLE

You set what you thought was a reasonable, attainable goal for one of your employees. But the staffer failed to meet the goal in the time you allotted. What do you do now? Follow these steps to bounce back:

- Take a balanced approach. Don't overreact. Assess the damage caused by not reaching the goal. That will help you look at things realistically.
- Figure out what went wrong. The best way to set the employee back on track is to make an honest effort to find out what derailed the staffer in the first place. Were there problems that you hadn't anticipated? Did you underestimate the time

needed to reach the goals? Did the employee lack resources or support?

- Revise the goal if you feel it was too ambitious. Don't fall prey to all-or-nothing thinking, believing that the staffer will never hit the targets. Break down your bigger aims into smaller ones that will be easier to achieve. Caution: if the employee continues to come up short, the problem may lie with the staffer, not the goal. Don't lower your standards or reduce the requirements of the job to accommodate a poor performer.

YOUR ATTITUDE IS SHOWING

We are the sum total of all our experiences. Every experience makes who we are at any given moment. It's not what happens to us in life that's important. What's important is how we perceive it and act. Remember when you get angry at someone for something said or done, you are really angry at yourself for not knowing how to cope with it.

The attitude you project affects your team, your colleagues, the overall image of the company or organization and ultimately the customer.

Everyone who has contact with customers – or, for that matter, anyone else working for the organization – has an effect on the way the company is perceived. We all exist as part of a total culture and we are all constantly supporting the culture either positively or negatively. An area for neutrality does not exist.

Your attitude about work and people is projected during work hours and at all other times. All contacts we have with the customer, or potential customer, shape and mold the customer's impression of the organization.

Personal success and the success of the company depend upon positive attitude. Further, maintaining a positive attitude can have a ripple effect on those you work with.

The attitude you have about people and work should be demonstrated in your behavior toward people at work.

LEADERSHIP IS NOT A RIGHT

The leader's positive attitude to do what's right is vital because leadership must be earned. It is not a right and once earned, must continue to be earned for the leader to be credible.

There have been occasions where a leader working in the family business participates in the development training. Oftentimes, in these situations, recognition needs to be given that though the position may be the result of the family connection; hard work is needed to both earn and maintain his/her role.

PROFESSIONAL DEVELOPMENT

Growing as a leader requires the adapting to other personalities and work environments. Although changing a position when our "self-esteem is in question" is not recommended, altering our view when it is not, oftentimes improves our development.

Here are a few behaviors that need a leader's attention and need to be avoided. How do you respond to each?

- Being too sure of self
- Providing too much detail
- Being too open
- Being obviously political
- Appearing wishy-washy
- Being indecisive
- Inability to handle what is asked of you

Professional posture

When communicating with the boss, be assertive, not non-assertive or aggressive. Let him/her know you are your own person and on the same page with the boss because he's usually right and you're in agreement. When disagreeing, do so firmly and identify how you feel about the issue and not in an aggressive manner.

INCREASE ASSERTIVENESS

Assertiveness is an important character trait of all effective leaders. Here are three key components to develop this need:

Confidence

- Make a plan for responding to situations that usually cause you stress. Practice your reaction in your mind. When the stressful situation occurs, take a deep, calming breath and follow through on what you rehearsed mentally. To stay calm and focused, concentrate on saying just enough to express your position.
- Develop strategies for dealing with disagreements. Instead of responding to someone's remarks, for example, just repeat what you've already said. Try to avoid unnecessary arguments with statements like "that may be true" or "we

see things differently, and let's work together to reach a solution."

Persistence

- Make a list of tasks or activities that you give up on too easily. Identify one or two to work on for a week. At the end of the week, grade yourself on your persistence with this scoring system: A = stuck to it, B = stayed focused most of the time, C = stayed on track some of the time, and D = gave up.
- Enlist a friend's help. Ask him or her to support you for a week, using reminders, requests, or encouragement to help you persist in your activities.

Decisiveness

- Draw up a list of all the unnecessary chores that others regularly ask you to do at work. Choose one or two to decline next week. Think of ways to politely, but firmly, say "no."
- Make a list of things you need other people to do for you in order to get your job done. Again, pick one or two and think about how you can make your request steadfastly but courteously.

BEING EFFECTIVELY ASSERTIVE

1. When expressing refusal, express a decisive "no." (You can explain why you are refusing; but there is no need to be defensive or overly apologetic). Don't hedge or leave the decision up to the other person.

2. Speak in an audible, firm tone of voice. Avoid being whiny or harsh and accusatory.

3. Give as prompt and brief a reply as possible, without unduly long pauses or interruptions.

4. Insist, where appropriate, on being treated with fairness and justice.

5. Request an explanation when being asked to do something unreasonable. Where appropriate, suggest a reasonable alternative.

6. Honestly express your feelings, without attacking or justifying yourself.

7. When expressing annoyance: tell the other person the aspects of his or her behavior you don't like; but don't attack the person, name-call, or accuse them.

OUR COMFORT ZONES

There are two kinds of people. Those who find pleasure in comfort and those who find pleasure in disturbing comfort zones. We cannot choose which one we are. It's pretty much the necessary component of our temperament.

Those who get pleasure in comfort need the comfort breakers to grow. Otherwise they would be content with who they are and what they do.

Each of us has had comfort breakers in our life. Someone who knew we could be and do much more. It could have been a parent, older sibling, teacher, or leader. These are the people we need to spend more time with.

Of course, we can get so content in our comfort zone that we don't want to change...it's our choice. Yet, when comfort zones are destroyed, poor habits are destroyed and replaced. Then life will become easier and also more satisfying.

GOOD AND POOR WORK NEEDS TO BE NOTICED. NOTICE GOOD WORK

- When you see it, say it
- Be specific and immediate
- Catch them doing something right
- Let them know how good it makes you feel
- Praise progress toward the desired goal
- Encourage them to do more of the same
- Provide positive reinforcement

NOTICE POOR WORK

- Make it private, make it positive
- Show them you care
- Ask questions, it might reveal information
- Offer simple, positive, and practical advice
- Be honest & direct, but be gentle
- Beware of defensive side tracks

THE STRUCTURE OF CHARACTER

In our relationship with others, we have to be careful to not judge character from background, education, and/or financial bearing.

Character structure makes an important contribution to the development of character and values. The more important human qualities may well be motivation, compassion, steadiness, perseverance, and the ability to put aside one's personal need for the good of the many, to sacrifice oneself for goals.

The person who is born brilliant, who spends his/her waking hours watching television is not likely to do much for the common good. A person can be born of modest means, yet with courage and wisdom, can make a significant contribution in work and life.

All are born equal and the circumstances of each person's environment varies, yet each of us can get inside ourselves and structure our character to do more for both ourselves and those we touch in the movement through our life.

TREAT YOURSELF WELL

We are the sum of all our experience. People treat us the way they see us treating ourselves. When you send out a good feeling, you get a good feeling back.

It's a fact that you get back exactly what you send out. This validates the concept that we can have whatever we want in life if we help other people get what they want.

Positive thinking will let you do more things better than negative thinking. Knowledge and positive energy help us to be more confident, which leads to enthusiasm. Enthusiasm is vital to doing and being more in your life.

REMEMBER: "WE'RE NOT WHAT WE THINK WE ARE, BUT WHAT WE THINK, WE ARE."

CHAPTER SEVEN

TEAM DYNAMICS

It is important for the worker to understand that he/she is valued and needed for the organization to reach its highest level of achievement.

We've heard the concept that "power corrupts and absolute power corrupts absolutely." It is natural because of our natural insecurities, to want to hang onto whatever power we can. Yet it is vital to be the best we can be as a leader to empower our people to be creative, to step forth boldly and let us know when they disagree.

WORKERS ARE EMPOWERED

The organization has reached the developmental stage when it becomes vitally important that workers understand what empowerment means and how it can be applied in the day-to-day work environment.

Traditional management has programmed today's worker to expect a dictatorial encounter and he/she needs to be coached to believe that a participatory leadership is in position. The conversion for the worker through coaching and the control of egos by management are the most important factors in this environmental change.

This change is highly necessary for organizations to grow in today's ever changing workplace. With empowerment providing ownership, which taps the creative and leadership skills of all workers, the full commitment and energy of the unit can be focused to meet goals and objectives.

Mixing workers in the right teams is important to ensure that all team members take roles in getting the job done. A team made up of quarterbacks is as ineffective as one made of guards or tackles.

Realize that building an ongoing team is a process. An effective procedure to develop teams is noted in the following program.

TEAMWORK CAN MAKE A DIFFERENCE

The word, teamwork, can be defined in many different ways. What needs to be present are mutual trust and respect. Without either, there can be no teamwork.

There are several things that can hurt the group's effort and prevent it from being a team. Two of the most common are:

1. Harmony is the prime objective to the extent that easy frankness in discussion is discouraged.
2. Formal hierarchical groups where members ratify the leaders' demands without challenge.

Ingredients that are important to well running teams are:

1. Clearly defined goals which are understood
2. Members have roles that impact on these goals

3. The goals are flexible as are the roles
4. Rewards are provided to compliment team successes
5. The leader is a coach who puts emphasis on process as well as content

PRINCIPLES THAT WORK

Leaders need to realize and communicate that the people who perform the work are the experts when it comes to solving problems in their areas.

They realize that the combined experience and talent of people working in teams are greater than those of anyone or any one individual. Experience shows that most people will take more active interest in a project if they can exert some influence upon the decisions that affect them.

All people have creative potential which can be systematically tapped through participation in a problem-solving group.

Workers who are not challenged to utilize the creativity will find other outlets such as involvement in sports and/or community activities.

LEADERS GROW BY MAKING THE FOLLOWING PART OF WHO THEY ARE

- Shut people out and they shut up. Bring people in and they open up
- Whatever you praise you cause to flower
- Opportunity is often inconvenient

- The power to define is the power to choose. Power resides not in aggressiveness but in conscious choice
- As you fix the problem you will not have to fix the blame
- Problems seldom exist at the level at which they are expressed
- Quieting the chattering mind promotes directed action

DON'T SET UP YOUR EMPLOYEES TO FAIL

Have you ever noticed what happens when a leader becomes dissatisfied with an employee's performance? Whether you realize it or not, you begin to create a "failure mindset." When people perceive chronic disapproval or lack of confidence and appreciation, they stop trying.

Here's what to avoid when managing an employee whose performance is slipping:

- **Don't go overboard with restrictions.**
  Be careful not to over manage an employee who has made some mistakes. Set up times to review performance without micromanaging. A troubled employee needs overseeing but it needs to be done in moderation.
- **Don't avoid face-to-face communication.**
  Avoid using email when confronting poor performance. In person or if necessary, by phone, verbally let the employee know what needs to be improved. Although not an easy task, speaking to an employee needing correction is a must and demonstrates your support. Following up a reprimand by email to confirm the contents of the meeting is additionally beneficial.
- **Don't lower your expectations.**
  When your employee's work doesn't meet your expectations, don't give him/her less challenging work. Except too little

and you'll get too little. Encourage the individual to know expectations with the coaching to support them. Challenge the works and let him/her know you expect to not be let down.

VALUE OTHERS TO GET POSITIVE RESULTS

1. Don't label others as dumb, cowardly, lazy, and childish or don't make sweeping judgments about feelings, especially about whether the feelings are real or important or morally right or wrong.
2. Have clear goals understood and agreed upon. Use the goals to test whether issues are relevant or not.
3. Don't make assumptions about how others think, feel, or react. You can't get inside anyone's head, and crystal-ball-gazing is for fortunetellers.
4. Be attentive to what you say – don't state your opinions as facts, don't use preaching words, and don't exaggerate or bulldoze others. Avoid absolute statements that leave no room for modification. "I think this is the way...," is better than "This is the only way..." Give people room to move.
5. Avoid sarcasm and kidding – they're ways of dirty fighting.
6. Listen empathically to others, stop yourself from working on counter-arguments while another person is speaking. Take the risk of being persuaded. Try the other person's reasoning "on for size."
7. Disagree or confront unrealistic or manipulative behavior but don't attack others as people.
8. Don't play manipulative games—be honest, direct, open, and specific. Don't correct statements of others about how they feel and don't tell them how they should feel.
9. Be careful of how you use questions—they are a demanding, controlling form of communications, especially the "Why?"

question. There is no scroll or script or engraved stone that says everybody must answer questions.

10. Don't be destructively generous. Let others exercise their right to be responsible for themselves.

11. If you are planning for others, provide some means for their involvement. The doers need to feel that they have influence on the decisions that affect them.

12. When you have differences, be willing to mediate any differences and work out contracts. When you do fight, <u>fight fairly</u>.

1. Set team-building objectives
2. Establish a positive climate for team building
3. Structure the process of team standards so they are clearly understood
4. Collect data on how effective the team is functioning
5. Establish criteria so efforts can be monitored
6. Identify blockages to work processes
7. Analyze why these blockages exist
8. Recognize, confront, and work through work blockages
9. Develop a shared vision of the future that will guide further team efforts
10. Establish concrete action plans

SELF-DIRECTED WORK TEAMS

Team members, after things get underway often make the same comments:

- Everyone seems to be going his/her own way
- We need guidelines to know what's going on
- We need specific direction

- Everyone is so busy that the team doesn't seem to be a priority
- Tell us the team's purpose

When the second phase is entered and implementation is key to growth, other questions need to be answered:

- Define our roles
- Make our objectives and performance expectations clearer
- Let's have scheduled work and more training

Another stage in development results in feelings being expressed as follows:

- Comfort zones are disturbed and reactions can be unpredictable
- What is the team's value? This becomes uncertain when personal duties need to fit in
- Previous supervisor's performances are compared to the present

A TEAM MUST DO IT FOR ITSELF

Neither an external nor an internal facilitator can make a team effective...the team just do it for itself. The facilitator can be the leader, coach, or consultant. The facilitator helps the team accomplish its objectives.

Facilitators should not:

1. Make decisions for the team
2. Become involved in content, but rather stay solely on process

3. Tell the team what's wrong with it, but help it recognize its own problems
4. Usurp leadership
5. Make the team dependent on his/her continued presence

The effective team puts importance on every member, realizing that the person doing the job is the expert. It knows that the effective work team improves quality, increases productivity, improves work habits, and is a cost saving.

The team-building concept identifies the following:

An excellent start for the second phase and the meetings that will be scheduled is to obtain feedback from the blockage questions team members are responding to. This study should make it possible for the team to increase its rate of progress.

Some effort must be taken to ensure that all of the teams are interfacing with one another...intra- and inter-department. This is important to ensure that the organization as a whole is on target and so teams can benefit from networking with one another.

HELP YOUR WORKERS SHINE

When you have a meeting with an upper-level executive or a key customer, invite a staff member along. Don't let the person just sit there, though. Assign him or her a meaningful role—presenting and explaining a section of the financial data under decision, for example.

Sentences that will help you grow and retain your best employees

Develop an arsenal of "openers" that you can use to keep your praise specific

"You really made a difference by…"

"I'm impressed with…"

"You got my attention with…"

"You're doing top quality work on …"

"You're right on the mark with…"

"One of the things I enjoy most about you is…"

"You can be proud of yourself for…"

We couldn't have done it without your…"

"What an effective way to…"

"You've made my day because of…"

CHAPTER EIGHT

Goal Setting

Long-term growth is a vital part of effective leadership. It's true that "if the organization doesn't have a clearly defined goal then any road will take it there."

Goals are more effectively attained when each employee is permitted to know that his/her role in the organization, is subject to development, and that its development is limited only by his/her contribution.

All employee decisions do not require leader approval. Decisions involve a balancing of risks and returns. Mistakes are inevitable and leaders need to know this and expect that employees will learn from their mistakes. It is the leader's role to watch their subordinates' long-term growth to be sure they learn knowing that successes increasingly outweigh their failures.

"While doing the smaller things, be sure that the bigger things are also being thought of to ensure that the small things are going in the right direction."

PATHS TO SUCCESS

Basic goals that need to be long-term:

- Encourage the creativity and energy of workers by training, empowering, and rewarding good performance
- Exceed customer expectations by going beyond
- Continuously improving by pursuing total quality as a way of who we are.

THE SOURCES OF SUCCESS

- Everyone is involved
- Hold brainstorming sessions
- Be sure our growth formula is fundamental
- Have ideas come from everyone and everywhere
- Let's reinvent what we have and who we are every year
- Encourage innovation at every level

FORMING THE RIGHT TEAM

Achievement is attained by images of success. Without positive images, achievement is not likely.

Successful individuals and organizations share an essential common denominator, their ability to utilize the power of high performance people.

Lead by teaching skills that release both individual and organization potential. Challenge old habits, beliefs, and attitudes that inhibit and block high performance and achievement. Provide ways to cut through barriers and translate potential into achievement. This effort overcomes resistance to change and sustains energy for success.

Individuals and organizations that set clear and challenging goals perform at higher levels than those who don't. This process helps in the setting of direction through specific and challenging training and development.

KEEPING PEOPLE WHO MAKE US SUCCESSFUL

As the economy improves, the need for leadership to put emphasis on keeping good employees becomes critical.

The retention process begins with selection, continues with making employees feel they belong in a participatory work climate, and continues even further when they're involved in team building—where they know they're important and not just a number.

WHY EMPLOYEES LEAVE

Employees leave their jobs when they lose confidence in the industry they're in, when there's a lack of appreciation and respect, when they're not being listened to and taken seriously, poor working conditions, when there's a lack of opportunity for advancement, and when compensation is inadequate.

WHAT GETS HIGH PRIORITY IN TODAY'S WORKFORCE

Autonomy is high on this list and is the feeling of belonging. Other items include the quality of life issues and a sense of community in the workplace.

RETAINING GOOD WORKERS

We can keep our good workers by providing each a personal growth plan, using creative recognition and reward, doing succession planning, by living the values expected, and making it easy for people to get their jobs done. Retaining people can also be enhanced by having an effective system to hire the right people to begin with.

A BOLD COMMITMENT

Both individuals and companies oftentimes are not as successful as they want and/or need to be not because they're moving in the wrong direction but because they're not moving boldly enough in any direction.

They need to ask "what is the single super goal or objective I/we must achieve to be more successful?"

Once deciding on what the goal or objective is then they're ready to commit to multiplying performance to exceed past performance and achieve on a grand scale what in the past seemed impossible. You can and will do this once you focus on defining and pursing your bold goal and/or objective.

NO EXCUSES-RESULTS

An organization would experience greater success by not accepting excuses. Excuses seem harmless but they are anything but harmless. They are linked to organizational problems. Excuses breed "Entitlement Thinking." When an excuse is offered, it is judged as acceptable or not acceptable. All excuses regardless of reason need to be not acceptable. In this way, people will find ways of doing rather than creating excuses for not doing.

This requires a culture change. It will require realizing that finding ways of doing is needed, and even though it will not remove all excuses, it will greatly reduce them and this in turn will improve the bottom line.

Where there are excuses, there will be undesirable results! The habit of excuse-making is the habit that is breeding entitlement thinking. It is the same habit that is killing American business!

When you eliminate excuses, you get rid of many other problems. When you get rid of the other problems, you make room for the positives. When you make room for the positive, you get results!

NOT GETTING EXCUSES

One reason people don't get results is because they are allowed to make excuses. Another reason people don't get results is because they are encouraged – almost "forced" by the system—to make excuses. When the system is set up in such a way that failure is inevitable, excuse-making is unknowingly encouraged in that company. This is because, given the choice between admitting to failure or making an excuse, most people most of the time will automatically give an excuse to spare themselves the pain. Again, excuses are an indicator, a warning signal, of a systematic problem (or problems) in the company. Where there are excuses, if we probe a bit, we will find other hidden problems. Excuses never travel alone.

Interestingly, positive and energetic people rarely make excuses, however, pessimistic people do. We won't eliminate pessimism in the workplace until we are rid of excuses. An excuse ridden culture can only be changed with proper leaders. Not leaders who play it safe to be more promotable but bold leaders who are more likely to ask for forgiveness rather than permission. Bold leaders will manage the change needed and examine the environment of the excuses, since the elimination of such begins and ends with acceptance by leadership.

It must be remembered that making excuses is an automatic and spontaneous response to avoid pain and criticism.

MAKING THE CHANGE

To make the change to an excuse free work environment, the leaders must be ready for the change, they must have a strong desire to win, and the commitment to do whatever it takes to excel. The culture is not determined by the organization's vision and mission but by its resolve to be the best. The value statement, "This organization will be an excuse free work environment" must be committed to.

Excuse making is the one common denominator of all management problems. When we get rid of excuses, we also get rid of our other problems. This is both significant and important to the change process, and will help maintain the momentum gained once the excuses turn to action and the problems turn into results.

THE CHANCE TO CREATE FIRE

Let's accept the fact that change has a destructive streak. It can rip the heart out of an organization. It can kill the spirit. At the very time an organization needs the best performance out of people, change often leaves job commitment lying wounded and weak. But change can be used to charge up the organization. That's because change opens up doors to people's hearts and minds that otherwise might stay forever locked.

The secret is to meet people at their point of need. You must manage to the moment…bring what's missing…repair what change has damaged or destroyed. And you need to move quickly, because high-velocity change puts heavy demands on the organization. You need people who invest themselves fully in their work, people, who deliver dramatic results.

Basically, it comes down to this—you need to build a burning level of job commitment, and you need to do it by yesterday. In today's world of work, you can't afford to tolerate a commitment level that remains at room temperature.

OVERCOMING THE CHALLENGE – I'M RESPONSIBLE

The challenge that most people face is that they know what they want, but oftentimes have a hard time focusing on the action steps to get there. It's difficult to have a long term focus when our lives are filled with diversions and distractions.

The key to overcoming this challenge is to make the commitment that you alone are responsible for your own life. Now we know that others and circumstances can cause our problem; however, when we can say and feel that "I'm responsible," we're in control.

It's not what happens to us in life that's important, what's important is how we perceive it. When I take responsibility, I can take the necessary steps to change and/or correct the situation. Otherwise, I have to wait for someone else to be responsible to take an action that I want.

CHAPTER NINE

MANAGING TIME EFFECTIVELY

When leaders and staff are asked to identify the principle limitation that prevents them from being even more effective in their job roles, the overwhelming answer is "lack of time."

Time is a complex phenomenon, a cultural development. Time is also a resource different than any other resource in that it uses itself. It requires constant awareness and good habits to maximize its use. Experts estimate that the average intellectual worker actually works at a 30% rate because of unintentionally wasting time. Good work habits result in working smarter, not harder.

The major difficulties in managing time come from not planning or setting objectives. Fear, tension, and indecisiveness are other difficulties.

To effectively utilize time, we need to be aware that it's a resource that must be guarded, for when it's misused, it's gone. Let's make the decision to be aware of bad habits, demands placed on our time by others, and spur of the moment activities that take us off course.

Without time management, the Parkinson's Law holds: "Work expands to fill the time available."

CONQUERING UNCOMMON TIME WASTERS

There are several common but seldom noticed time wasters which need to be stopped to handle time effectively.

When a co-worker says something derogatory, don't respond in kind but rather take a mental step back and thank the person for the feedback. Think on it, decide if it's legitimate, and act accordingly.

When you get bored with what you're doing, try to delegate routine tasks to others who may be more interested or suited to those kinds of tasks or activities.

Be careful not to say "yes" too often. You could be seen as a helpful person yet be wasting a lot of time to every request you receive. Ask if the task supports your goals and if not, decline diplomatically.

MAXIMIZING TIME

Many people think of themselves as procrastinators but oftentimes, they are not. The key to the effective utilization of time is to use the strategies that work for you and your unique situations, thereby creating your own system. Simple strategies almost always work best.

We can improve our time by checking our calendar first thing, planning on keeping distractions to a minimum, and work at keeping as much as possible in one place. It's best to implement this system on work days only.

As a leader, you're responsible for the efficient use of resources given to you: personnel, dollars, space, and equipment. There is one resource that is strictly limited, your own time. No act of any kind can alter that. Your time is a precious resource which needs to be effectively utilized for you to be successful. Good time management benefits your organization and you.

Common time wasters

A leader may appear to be busy all day; yet a close study of what is being done often shows that a good deal of time is being wasted, in these ways:

1. Trying to do everything
2. Socializing too much
3. Building an image (Working through lunches, vacations, etc.)
4. Scheduling too much time for a task (Recall Parkinson)
5. Failing to set priorities
6. Putting off tasks which are distasteful
7. Permitting interruptions

BE OPEN TO SUGGESTIONS

Leaders can improve their time management by utilizing an employee suggestion program. It gets employees involved, gives them a sense of importance, and they'll do more, saving the leader time.

Keys to creating an atmosphere where employees feel willing to volunteer their ideas and suggestions are vital.

First describe the suggestions you're looking for. Employees will respond better to well-defined categories that help them frame their thinking and target their creative efforts. Categories might include such things as safety, cost savings, and customer service.

Then demonstrate the process by letting employees know what will happen to any ideas suggested. A flow chart that shows the approval and review process will take the mystery out of the program. Also, give workers a general idea of how long a typical response will take.

Last, designate an advocate. A high-profile leader with good employee rapport can keep the program moving. The advocate should have a location to record the ideas, encourage workers to submit their ideas, and coach them. Plus, the advocate should help move ideas through the pipeline and clear away obstacles when they occur.

GOOD TIME MANAGEMENT REQUIRES BEING ABLE TO CHANGE

Every day presents a new opportunity. Oftentimes we're unable to seize the moment because we're mired in old habits, doing the same thing over and over again. Some people believe that they can't change and say, "That's just the way I am." You can change. You can start now. It could change your life today and you don't have to wait for July 1.

We tend to stay in routines, our comfort zones, regardless of how useful the routine is. Experiences have shown that the more we do something, the more the habit grows. We get into a groove with the longer the habit, the more difficult it is to change. But we can change. We can form new habits that are better for us, that would help us grow. Sure change is hard, but change is life. Ask yourself, if I change the way I do something will I be an entirely different person or will I be just interacting differently? Remember, no one is perfect. Be bold enough to step up to what you want to do, want to be, and do it now and in not a long time, the new way will be the old way.

CHAPTER TEN

MAKING DECISIONS AND
SOLVING PROBLEMS

The better argument doesn't necessarily win, the presentation makes the difference. Success comes to those who are more effective in process. That's the reason why those who package themselves and things effectively are accepted more readily than those with the better product or idea that are lacking in presentation skills.

Both individuals and organizations oftentimes are not as successful as they want, need, and/or are capable of being not because they're moving in the wrong direction but because they're not moving boldly enough in any direction.

The leader's concern about making a bad decision results in decisions not being made or worse, being made with less than the boldness needed to be accepted. Oftentimes the less than the best decision is accepted and effectively implemented because of the positive way it is presented.

Risk-Taking Concept

It is generally known that risk-taking can provide the "creative edge" and increase productivity and job satisfaction, yet leaders do not encourage it because costly learning experiences are difficult to explain to results-oriented top management.

Growth is related to risk-taking, and moderate risk-taking provides goals that are both challenging and realistic. The realistic aspect increases the possibility of success and builds confidence that the goal is achievable.

One of the marks of an effective leader is the ability to make sound decisions. Leaders are called upon to make decisions concerning a wide variety of matters. Some of the simple issues can be handled quickly and easily; yet others require a considerable amount of careful thought and study before the decisions can be reached.

The well-known six-step approach to effective decision-making has been found to be a good personalized approach. The steps listed are normally followed in the order presented although the sequence is not rigid. This approach is only as beneficial as clear thinking and sound judgment accompany it to be.

The steps are as follows:

Step 1: State the problem
Step 2: Define the situation
Step 3: Assemble and evaluate data
Step 4: Develop possible solutions
Step 5: Select the solutions
Step 6: Plan the implementation and follow-up

Problems can generally be more effectively resolved when management involves their workers in the decision-making. Leaders recognize the "buck stops with them." However, that doesn't remove the value of getting workers involved in the decisions.

When workers are asked their opinions, they feel part of what's going on and will make commitments to following through on making what is decided is successful, even when their suggestions were not utilized. Being asked to be involved gives them the so important need to feel like they belong.

CREATIVE WORKERS

It's been stated that the worker is only as good as the perception and expectations of his/her leader. Most workers are creatively underutilized. That's the reason so many workers volunteer their creative abilities in in the communities as little league coaches, den mothers, and PTA leaders. Although their efforts are beneficial, they give insight into their jobs not being challenging enough.

An effective organization finds ways to capture the creativity in the workplace. Leaders need to be encouraged to control their egos and insecurities alike; to invite workers into the decision-making process by communicating horizontally rather than vertically. This removes the "do it because I said so" impression.

WHEN DISAGREEING – REFRAME THE DISCUSSION

When you want to persuade someone you're disagreeing with begin by taking a point of view you both agree with. This will signal to the other person that you're not just looking for an argument.

In honest disagreement both individuals want good results rather than conflict. With the facts in front of you, the two of you can respectfully provide your positions. Even when agreement isn't reached, you never would have gotten to this point without effectively listening to one another.

LETTING GO TO GROW

We need to learn to live with mindful presence in the moment. Communicate by being unhampered by judgment, have no plan to fix or change him or her, or have personal projections. Some people will like us and some dislike us; some come through for us and some betray us; some care tenderly about our feelings and some trample them underfoot. Accepting this variety as a given makes it less likely that we will let the reactions of others determine our personal worth.

Our desires and fears from the past are recorded in the cells of our bodies. We keep looking for the love we missed. We keep fearing a repetition of what we can't forget.

It is through letting go that one grows. If you need to hang on to it, you prove that you really don't own it. So we grow by learning to "let go to grow." To shed shells, create vacuums so things of greater value can take its place.

CHANGING OUR DECISION-MAKING WORK ENVIRONMENT

By moving from a dictatorial to participatory leadership style, the work environment begins developing a vision of greatness that verbalizes the future that is wished for. The vision needs to be both strategic and innovative. Strategic to stay focused on customers and users to express a benefit to the organization's mission. It also needs to be innovative to capture imagination and spirit.

The vision needs to be continually communicated to keep others on target. The more it's talked about, the more committed we become.

The culture's direction is enhanced when workers are encouraged to share their own visions of greatness. They need to be helped to develop a personal, clear, and specific vision statement that identifies their responsibility.

It is easier and natural to do things as they've always been done. Not to fix something that needs fixing until it is broken. This can cause us to lose our visions. It takes courage to commit and stick to a vision of greatness. Yet, it's the best way for the organization to grow for it is through involvement that the worker is happiest, it is through the happiest worker that the organization experiences success, and through organizational success that results in the corporate culture being realized.

Let's remember that it's not what happens to us in life that's important, what's important is how we perceive it. We are the sum total of all our experiences and "we're not what we think we are, but what we think, we are."

When one believes and states that it can't be done, he/she is right. If the person believes and states that it can be done, the answer is the same. The Law of Expectations is real.

In "Think and Grow Rich," Napoleon Hill states, "What the mind conceives and believes becomes reality." This needs to be changed to state, what the mind can conceive and believe is reality."

It is time for leaders to step up and be what they can be. For them to recognize that their limitations are within their own perception.

Organizations are better led by those who are bolder, more willing to take risks, rather than those who might be more capable but are more adverse to risk taking. So stop talking and thinking about what you're going to do and confidently move forward now in doing it. A good leader first takes control of self and then the situation needing attention.

EPILOGUE

The book was written because of the author's concern about where we are going as a people. Values and integrity have been lessened in favor of lying and cheating, which are being more readily accepted.

It seems that 80% of the people are going through life waiting for it to happen while only 20% are making it happen. Lack of accountability in work environments that are full of excuses is commonplace.

Great leaders tend to routinely break the rules. They assess conventional wisdom about human nature and leading people, turning it upside down. Great leaders are neither passive nor aggressive but bold. They are bold enough to be specific in direction while letting those responsible to them know they are open to disagreement and questioning. That communication, to be effective, needs to be horizontal. Communication should be equal with respect for each other's position.

To better our weak environment and the world as a whole, we need to do what is right, not for fear of being caught, but rather because it is the right thing. Remember each of us is an individual soul with an individual mission so follow your desires and inspire others to live their best life. Do not allow anyone to stop you singing the song in your soul and expressing the unique gifts you were born with. Your passions and desires are important to your youthfulness and health so create a job that makes you feel joyful. Your life will be richer in so many ways if you follow your passion instead of just going through life waiting for it to happen. Set your powerful intention and get ready for increase. Keep believing, keep following God's laws, and keep your heart and mind open for your Law of Attraction to kick in. We were born to co-create and cooperate. The universe is supremely abundant and full of energy that is ready to support you, so release your fear and fill the lack inside of you with hope.

We need to accept the concept that the "Time is Now." We are the sum total of all our experiences and we are nothing more than what we perceive we are. Become part of the 20% that recognize that "We're not what we think we are, but rather what we think, we are."

www.ingramcontent.com/pod-product-compliance
Lightning Source LLC
Chambersburg PA
CBHW050420290526
45786CB00003B/1340